Quotes 365
Thought Provoking Quotes for Every Day of the Year

April Scales

Cadmus Publishing
www.cadmuspublishing.com

Copyright © 2022 April Scales

Published by Cadmus Publishing
www.cadmuspublishing.com
Port Angeles, WA

ISBN: 978-1-63751-364-4

All rights reserved. Copyright under Berne Copyright Convention, Universal Copyright Convention, and Pan-American Copyright Convention. No part of this book may be reproduced, stored in a retrieval system, or transmitted in any form, or by any means, electronic, mechanical, photocopying, recording or otherwise, without prior permission of the author.

This book is dedicated to Stacy and everyone who believed that my words could change lives.

1

IF YOU WERE PERFECT, I WOULDN'T WANT YOU

2

Your start is the day that you know that you need to make a change

3

IT IS FREE TO MIND YOUR BUSINESS

4

LAWS WITHOUT MORALS ARE USELESS

5

Don't Ruminate...Illuminate!

6

INDULGE IN THE POSITIVE

7

IF THE PACKAGE LOOKS DAMAGED, CHANCES ARE THE CONTENTS ARE TOO. PROCEED WITH CAUTION

8

BUILD YOUR MENTAL MUSCLE

9

LEAD AN ABUNDANT LIFE BY CLEANING OUT THE NEGATIVE INFLUENCES

10.

DEFIANCE IS MY MIDDLE NAME

11.

MOTHER NATURE IS A WOMAN THAT DESERVES RESPECT

12.

BEST FRIENDS STAY IN TOUCH

13.

WHEN SOMEONE OFFERS YOU A PIECE OF GUM, TAKE IT!

14.

I AM ENOUGH FOR ME

15.

BAD DAYS MAY BEND ME, BUT THEY WILL NOT BREAK ME

16.

I WILL REINVENT MYSELF TODAY

17.

GOD MADE ME WITH LOVE

18.

I DESERVE ONE GUILTY PLEASURE

19.

UNLOCK YOUR UNIQUE

20.

YOU ARE BOLD AND BEAUTIFUL!

21.

I LOVE MY BODY, FLAWS AND ALL

22.

YOU CANNOT CAN ME OUT OF MY CONFIDENCE

23.

YOU ARE AMAZING JUST THE WAY YOU ARE

24.

COMPETITION BUILDS CONFIDENCE

25.

I AM INFALLIBLE

26.

MIND OVER MATTER. IF YOU DON'T MIND, IT DOESN'T MATTER

_____
_____
_____
_____
_____
_____
_____
_____
_____
_____
_____
_____
_____
_____
_____
_____
_____
_____

27.

I AM THE RULER OF THIS ROOST!

28.

I AM NOT A PAIR OF JEANS, YOU WILL NEVER LABEL ME

29.

S.T.O.P. (SIT DOWN, THINK ABOUT IT, OBSERVE, PRAY)

30.

GET COMFORTABLE WITH BEING UNCOMFORTABLE

31.

IF IT DOESN'T CONCERN YOU, IT JUST DOESN'T CONCERN YOU

32.

THE LOUDEST DOG RARELY BITES

33.

YOU CAN NEVER ELEVATE TO MY LEVEL

34.

DON'T DO SOMETHING "JUST FOR TODAY", DO IT FOR TOMORROW AS WELL

35.

OWN THE YOU SEE IN THE MIRROR

36.

GENERATE KINDNESS TODAY

37.

EMPOWER YOURSELF AND OTHERS WITH LOVE

38.

DON'T LET YOUR EXTERNALS CHANGE YOUR INTERNALS

___
___
___
___
___
___
___
___
___
___
___
___
___
___
___
___
___
___

39.

APPRECIATE YOUR LOVED ONES BEFORE THEY DEPRECIATE YOU FROM THEIR LIVES

40.

YOU ARE WORTHY, NOT WORTHLESS

41.

DON'T LET YOUR FEAR OVERRUN YOUR COURAGE

42.

THE HARDEST STORY TO TELL IS YOUR OWN

43.

THE ONLY HIGH YOU NEED IS ADRENALINE

44.

MY HEART COMES WITH THE STICKER "FRAGILE", DO NOT BREAK

45.

WISDOM IS YOUR YOUTH TO LOSE, AND A TIME JUST TO PLAY THE GAME FOR FUN

46.

THERE IS A TIME TO WIN, A TIME TO LOSE, AND A TIME JUST TO PLAY THE GAME FOR FUN

47.

IT NEVER FEELS BETTER TO HAVE LOVED AND LOST THAN NEVER TO HAVE LOVED AT ALL

48.

MY LOVE FOR YOU IS LIKE THE SUN...EFFERVESCENT

49.

NEGATIVITY IS LIKE A CANCER; IT CAN POTENTIALLY KILL YOU

50.

TREAT LIFE LIKE A CHECKBOOK AND FIND YOUR BALANCE

51.

BAD FRIENDS ARE LIKE SPLIT ENDS, CUT THEM, AND THROW THEM AWAY

52.

OPTIONS ARE GREAT, NEVER RELINQUISH YOURS

53.

DAYS ARE LIKE VARIABLES IN MATH, THEY CAN GO EITHER WAY

54.

DO YOU EVER FEEL LIKE A RED BRICK IN A WHITE WALL?

55.

THE TRUE ANSWER LIES WITHIN

56.

WHEN YOU TRULY KNOW YOURSELF, YOU WILL NEVER BE LONELY

_____
_____
_____
_____
_____
_____
_____
_____
_____
_____
_____
_____
_____
_____
_____
_____
_____

57.

WHEN YOU APOLOGIZE FOR THE SAME ACT MORE THAN ONCE, YOU MEANT TO DO IT IN THE FIRST PLACE

58.

HOW MUCH BEAUTY DO YOU BEHOLD?

59.

NEW THINGS CAN BE SCARY TO LEARN, BUT THEY ARE NECESSARY FOR GROWTH

60.

RAINWATER CLEANSES THE EARTH; CRYING CLEANSES YOUR SOUL

61.

IF YOU WROTE A DEFINITION OF YOURSELF, WHAT WOULD IT SAY?

62.

YOU CAN'T CONTROL THE WEATHER, BUT YOU CAN CONTROL YOUR TONGUE

63.

ALWAYS TELL THE TRUTH, YOUR HONOR IS AT STAKE

64.

YOU NEVER KNOW WHAT YOU CAN GET THROUGH UNTIL YOU LOOK BACK AND SEE THAT YOU'VE GOTTEN THROUGH IT

65.

PROCRASTINATION THROWS YOU FARTHER BEHIND

66.

YOUR ACTIONS ARE THE CAUSE OF ANOTHER PERSON'S REACTIONS

_____
_____
_____
_____
_____
_____
_____
_____
_____
_____
_____
_____
_____
_____
_____
_____
_____

67.

MANAGE YOUR TIME WISELY. LIFE IS TOO SHORT TO WASTE

68.

THE MIND IS LIKE A RUBBER BAND; IT COULD SNAP AT ANY MOMENT

69.

You don't know what you're missing unless you've had it

70.

HATRED AND RACISM ARE LIKE CIGARETTES; THEY ARE BOTH DETRIMENTAL TO YOUR HEALTH

71.

LAUGHTER IS THE BEST MEDICINE. DON'T FORGET YOUR DAILY DOSE

72.

IF YOU THINK YOU'RE IN COMPLETE CONTROL, YOU ARE CRAZIER THAN YOU THINK

73.

ALLOW SILENCE TO CALM YOUR MIND

74.

You cannot explore the world with a closed mind

75.

YOU DON'T HAVE TO BEND OVER BACKWARDS, BUT YOU DO HAVE TO REMAIN FLEXIBLE

76.

DON'T ALLOW YOUR RESENTMENTS TO HOLD YOU BACK

77.

BEAUTY REFLECTS YOUR PERCEPTION OF THINGS

78.

TOSS YOUR FEARS OUT WITH THE TRASH

79.

OBSERVATION LEADS TO EDUCATION

80.

ALL WORK AND NO PLAY EQUAL A BORING LIKE

81.

ACTION + REACTION = CONSEQUENCE. THINK BEFORE YOU ACT

82.

COMPASSION CAN BE THERAPEUTIC

83.

STOP MAKING EXCUSES AND DITCH AT LEAST ONE HABIT

84.

SEX IS LIKE MEDICATION, IT COMES WITH A WARNING AND SIDE EFFECTS

85.

OPPORTUNITIES OCCUR WHEN YOU STEP OUTSIDE OF YOUR COMFORT ZONE

86.

DON'T WAIT UNTIL A RAINY DAY TO FIX THE ROOF

87.

IF YOU SAVE YOUR PENNIES, THE DOLLARS WILL TAKE CARE OF THEMSELVES

88.

SOMETIMES YOU MUST AGREE TO DISAGREE

89.

Wake up wanting to be the best possible version of yourself

90.

WHATEVER YOU ARE GOING THROUGH, CONTINUE TO GO UNTIL IT IS BEHIND YOU

91.

A CHILD IS NOT A MISTAKE, IT IS AN EXAMPLE OF GOD'S OWN PURPOSE

92.

YOU WILL GAIN SO MUCH MORE WHEN YOU LEARN TO LIVE WITH LESS

93.

TREAT YOUR BODY AS A TEMPLE AND IT WILL WORSHIP YOU IN THE END

94.

LISTEN TO YOUR BODY, IT WILL LET YOU KNOW WHEN IT NEEDS A TUNE UP

95.

INNER BEAUTY NEVER DIES

96.

YOU CAN MEND A BROKEN NAIL, BUT YOU CANNOT MEND A BROKEN PROMISE

97.

TO KNOW THEN WHAT I KNOW NOW WOULD MAKE ME A GENIUS

98.

WHEN YOU HAVE NO LIMITS, YOU ARE DESTINED TO GO OVER THE EDGE

99.

IF WE WEREN'T SUPPOSED TO BE JUDGMENTAL, WHY WERE WE GIVEN THE ABILITY TO JUDGE?

100.

A HOUSE IS NOT THE SAME AS A HOME

101.

You are model even when you are not on the runway

102.

EVEN ADULTS OCCASIONALLY NEED A "TIME OUT"

103.

NO TWO COOKIES ARE CUT THE SAME, ONE WILL ALWAYS RISE HIGHER THAN THE OTHER

104.

PEOPLE ARE LIKE SIEVES, YOU GOTTA SIFT THROUGH THEM

105.

DON'T PLAY DUMB OR YOUR ACT MAY BECOME REALITY

106.

IT'S OKAY TO STUMBLE OR FALL BUT IT'S NOT OKAY TO STAY THERE

107.

GOOD THINGS MAY COME TO THOSE WHO WAIT BUT GOOD THINGS COME FASTER WHEN YOU GO AFTER THEM

108.

RUN TOWARDS LOVE, WALK AWAY FROM HATE

109.

TIME DOESN'T ALWAYS HEAL ALL WOUNDS

110.

EAT BECAUSE ITS NUTRITIOUS, NOT BECAUSE IT'S DELICIOUS

111.

PRAYER IS AS BASIC AS ABC. ASK AND YOU SHALL RECEIVE

112.

RELATIONSHIPS ARE LIKE CANDLES; YOU CANNOT BURN THEM AT BOTH ENDS

113.

Work with what you have and make it into what you want

114.

LIFE IS LIKE A STORY; IT HAS A BEGINNING, MIDDLE, AND END

115.

HOW CAN WE ACHIEVE BALANCE WHEN WE VIEW THINGS ONE-SIDED?

116.

DEATH WOULDN'T BE SO BAD IF IT WASN'T PERMANENT

117.

THE MIND IS LIKE A LIGHT SWITCH, IT CUTS OFF, ON, AND FLICKERS

118.

BEGIN EACH DAY WITH A 24-HOUR PURPOSE

119.

DON'T LET YOUR TONGUE BE THE DEATH OF YOU

120.

YOU CAN HAVE THE LAST WORD WITH SILENCE

121.

WHAT IF I COULD REMEMBER EVERYTHING I'VE FORGOTTEN?

122.

LET YOUR STRENGTHS OVERTHROW YOUR WEAKNESSES

123.

HONESTLY SPEAKING, EVERYONE HAS SOME FORM OF PREJUDICE

124.

HANG YOUR RACK R.(RANDOM) A.(ACTS)C.(CARING) AND K. (KINDNESS) FOR THE WORLD TO SEE

125.

ALL YOU NEED IS TO FEEL SAFE AND STABLE

126.

SURVIVAL IS NEVER AN OPTION. IT IS THE ONLY CHOICE

127.

GIVE AWAY ALL OF THE LOVE THAT YOU WANT TO RECEIVE

128.

YOU POSSESS ALL OF THE TOOLS YOU NEED IN ORDER TO BUILD SOMETHING GREAT

129.

WHEN PEOPLE ENVY YOU, IT MEANS THAT YOU'RE DOING SOMETHING RIGHT

130.

A COMPLIMENT CAN GO A LONG WAY

131.

CONFUSION MEANS THAT YOU NEED TO STOP AND TAKE A BREATH

132.

I DO HAVE A SHAPE. ISN'T ROUND ONE OF THEM?

133.

YEAH ME!! BE YOUR OWN CHEERLEADER!!

134.

IS BEING STUBBORN A PERMANENT TRAIT?

135.

EVERYTHING BROKEN CANNOT BE FIXED

136.

I WAS LUCKY ENOUGH TO BE CHOSEN ONE

137.

THE ONES THAT DIDN'T THINK I'D SUCCEED MOTIVATED ME HARDER THAN THE ONES WHO KNEW I WOULD

138.

WILL YOUR ACTIONS LIMIT YOU OR LIBERATE YOU?

139.

HAVE YOU EVER OPENED YOUR MOUTH AND REGRETTED IT?

140.

UPGRADE YOUR FEMININITY/ MASCULINITY

141.

THE LAST TIME THAT I THOUGHT I WAS RIGHT, I WAS WRONG

142.

HUMILITY IS A BEAUTIFUL CHARACTERISTIC

QUOTES 365

143.

CHEATERS DON'T CHANGE

144.

BE YOUR CHILD'S SUPERHERO

145.

YOU DEAL WITH THE HAND LIFE DEALS YOU. SOMETIMES YOU WIN, SOMETIMES YOU LOSE, AND SOMETIMES YOU'VE GOTTA CALL IT A DRAW

146.

A BROKEN MIND CANNOT HEAL ON ITS OWN

147.

EVERY CUT CANNOT BE COVERED WITH A BAND-AID

148.

BITING YOUR TONGUE CAN BE VERY PAINFUL AT TIMES

149.

WISDOM WILL COME....JUST GIVE IT TIME

150.

WHAT YOU WANT ISN'T ALWAYS WHAT YOU NEED

151.

NO IS ALWAYS AN OPTION

152.

TEARS ARE THE RIVERS OF LIFE, DON'T BE AFRAID TO LET THEM FLOW

153.

TIME ISN'T FOR SALE

154.

YOU CANNOT PLACE A HALF BET; IT'S ALL OR NOTHING

155.

YOU'LL NEVER FIND WHAT YOU NEED IF YOU STOP LOOKING

156.

You don't need coercion to do a good deed

157.

REACHING THE MOUNTAIN TOP IS NOT AS IMPORTANT AS THE CLIMB

158.

DON'T ALLOW YOUR CRUTCHES TO CRIPPLE YOU FOR LIFE

159.

CLOSENESS ONLY COUNTS IN HORSES AND HAND GRENADES

160.

THERE'S ALWAYS ONE WHO'S NOT GOING TO LIKE THE PERSON YOU'VE BECOME

161.

PROBLEMS ARE LIKE FLAT TIRES, IF YOU DON'T FIX THEM, YOU'LL NEVER REACH YOUR DESTINATION

162.

IF YOU REACH PERFECTION, THEN YOU HAVE NOTHING TO AIM FOR

163.

ALTHOUGH PRAYERS ARE DONE IN THE DARK, WE OFTEN SEE THE ANSWERS IN THE LIGHT

164.

OUR TRUE FRIENDS SEE OUR FLAWS BEFORE WE DO AND STILL LIKE US

165.

POSSIBILITIES ARE LIMITLESS

166.

Your potential holds no boundaries

167.

RELEASE THE VICES THAT HAVE A HOLD ON YOU

168.

YOU CAN FIND SERENITY AMONG CHAOS. LOOK INSIDE YOURSELF FOR PEACE

169.

THERE'S NEVER A WINNER IN THE WAR OF WORDS

170.

NEVER BEGIN THE DAY IN A BAD MOOD

171.

MEMORIES ONLY HAPPEN ONCE IN A LIFETIME

172.

STAYING ANGRY IS A WASTE OF AN EMOTION

173.

IF IDEAS WERE LIGHTBULBS, HOW BRIGHT WOULD YOUR WORLD BE?

174.

REVERE THOSE WHO RAISED YOU, THEY DIDN'T HAVE TO DO IT

175.

DISCIPLINE COMES FROM THE DESIRE TO DO BETTER

176.

DON'T INSULT MY INTELLIGENCE WITH YOUR STUPIDITY!

177.

THE QUESTION WAS WALKED BEFORE YOU SOFTENED YOUR PATH

178.

THOSE WALKED BEFORE YOU SOFTENED YOUR PATH

179.

YOU MAY NOT BE THE ONE WHO DISCOVERS YOUR GIFTS/TALENTS

180.

You cannot plant the seed of wisdom

181.

DREAMS DO NOT ONLY COME TRUE WHEN YOU'RE ASLEEP

182.

LYING ONLY BUYS TIME FOR MORE LIES

183.

OUR FORKED PATHS WILL EVENTUALLY CROSS

184.

MY EYES MAY BE CLOSED BUT MY EARS ARE OPEN

185.

MISERY DOESN'T LOVE COMPANY, IT JUST NEEDS A HUG

186.

NO HAS FEWER LETTERS THAN YES

187.

WHY DO WE CRY AT WEDDING AND FUNERALS?

188.

I DON'T ALWAYS TRY TO UNDERSTAND YOUR POINT OF VIEW

189.

TEACH BY EXAMPLE

190.

WHEN YOU'RE PUSHED INTO A CORNER, COME OUT SWINGING

191.

BRING REVENGE WITH KINDNESS

192.

CONTRARY TO BELIEF, NOT EVERY IDEA IS A GOOD ONE

193.

FIND YOUR NICHE. YOU ARE GOOD AT SOMETHING

194.

DO NOT BURN BRIDGES, THEY ARE TOO HARD TO REBUILD

195.

Harsh Words Hurt Worse Than Sticks and Stones

196.

YOUR LOVE IS MORE PRECIOUS THAN GOLD, TOO BAD I PREFER SILVER

197.

DON'T ALLOW THE CRACK IN YOUR FOUNDATION TO GET TOO BIG TO FIX

198.

Your reflection in the mirror speaks volumes

_____
_____
_____
_____
_____
_____
_____
_____
_____
_____
_____
_____
_____
_____
_____
_____

199.

REAPING ALWAYS SHOWS THE SEEDS THAT YOU PLANTED

200.

INSECURITIES ARE BAD FIRST IMPRESSIONS

201.

Your character is judged by your work and your word

202.

IF YOU AREN'T GOOD AT LYING, DON'T!

203.

THE TONGUE IS SHARPER THAN THE SWORD

204.

BE MINDFUL OF THE LEGACY THAT YOU WILL LEAVE BEHIND

205.

TEMPTATIONS ARE OFTEN SUBTLE

206.

MARRIAGES ARE LIKE LAYAWAYS; THEY HAVE A RETURN POLICY CALLED DIVORCE

207.

I'M GIVING YOU MY LOVE. I WANT YOU TO KEEP IT SAFE

208.

I DON'T DO HE SAID/SHE SAID. GIVE IT TO ME STRAIGHT OR KEEP IT TO YOURSELF

209.

NOW THAT I SEE THINGS CLEARLY, I'VE DECIDED THAT I JUST DON'T LIKE YOU!

210.

ACCEPT ME AS I AM OR TAKE A HIKE!

211.

THERE'S NO COMPARISON TO YOU AND ME... I'M JUST BETTER

212.

I CAME OUT A DARK BECAUSE YOU SHOWED ME THE LIGHT

213.

MEASURE YOUR WORTH IN BLESSINGS

214.

YOUR GUT FEELING IS USUALLY RIGHT, UNLESS ITS GAS

215.

WHAT IS IMPORTANT TO YOU EMPOWERS YOU

216.

AS A HUMAN, I WILL ERR

217.

IT'S ONLY ARROGANT WHEN YOU CANNOT BACK UP WHAT YOU SPEAK

218.

IT DOESN'T TAKE MUCH TO START A FIRE, BUT IT DOES TO REKINDLE A FLAME

219.

WARRIORS FIGHT OUR BATTLES. WHEN THEY ARE WOUNDED, WHO FIGHTS FOR THEM

220.

WE ARE ALL RELATED IN THE COMMUNITY OF LIFE

221.

HOW ARE ALL RELATED IN THE COMMUNITY OF LIFE?

222.

HATERS ONLY GET ALONG WITH OTHER HATERS

223.

THE MORE YOU APPRECIATED THE VALUE OF OTHERS THE LESS YOU DEPRECIATE YOUR OWN

224.

RESPECT CAN ONLY BE RECIPROCATED WHEN IT'S GIVEN

225.

SOMETIMES ALL WE NEED IS A KICK IN THE ASS TO GET US MOVING

226.

I'VE ONLY MADE ONE MISTAKE... YOU

227.

I MAY LIVE A LIFETIME AND NEVER UNWRAP ALL OF MY GIFTS

228.

NOT ALL STATEMENTS NEED AN ENDING

229.

IF YOU JUDGE ME BY THE COLOR OF MY SKIN, MY COLOR IS OPAQUE

230.

EXCLUSION FROM ONE GROUP MEANS INCLUSION OF ANOTHER

231.

GOOD PEOPLE HAVE BAD THOUGHTS

232.

BREAKDOWNS DON'T JUST OCCUR ON THE SIDE OF THE ROAD

233.

DOCTORS AREN'T THE ONLY HEALERS

234.

ANCHORS ARE THE ONLY THINGS THAT NEED TO BE WEIGHED DOWN

235.

MY HEART AWAKENS WHEN YOU SMILE

236.

TOLERANCE IS A TRAIT THAT I DO NOT POSSESS

237.

WASTING TIME IS LIKE WASTING MONEY, EVENTUALLY YOU WILL RUN OUT OF BOTH

238.

Your name is not sun, the world does not revolve around you

239.

THERE IS BEAUTY IN MANY THINGS, YOU'RE JUST NOT ONE OF THEM

240.

DEBRIS SHOULD'VE BEEN YOUR NAME BECAUSE YOU'RE NOTHING BUT TRASH!

241.

FINDING BALANCE LEADS TO INNER PEACE

242.

OIL AND WATER DON'T MIX WELL AND NEITHER DO WE!

243.

DISTRACTIONS OFTEN LEAD TO DISASTERS

244.

THOSE WHO CAN SING SHOULD. THOSE WHO CAN'T... SHOULDN'T

245.

THE TRUTH COULD SET YOU FREE IF YOU SPOKE IT

246.

SOMETIMES YOU REACH THE AGE AT WHICH YOU JUST DON'T CARE AND HERE I AM

247.

IF THIS IS THE LAND OF THE FREE, WHY DO WE PAY TAXES?

248.

IF I'M WHOLE, WHY DO I NEED A BETTER HALF?

249.

ALL GOOD THINGS MUST COME TO AN END, SO… GOODBYE

250.

WHY ARE THE DUMBEST PEOPLE ALWAYS THE LOUDEST?

251.

TALK IS CHEAP, WHAT ARE YOU WORTH?

252.

IF I INTERRUPT YOU, I'M OBVIOUSLY NOT INTERESTED IN WHAT YOU HAVE TO SAY

253.

EVEN A FALLEN STAR CAN SHINE BRIGHT

254.

I SPEAK ALOUD WHAT OTHERS THINK IN SILENCE

255.

SQUARES DO NOT FIT IN MY CIRCLE

256.

IF YOU PRACTICED WHAT YOU PREACH, WHAT WOULD YOUR SERMON BE?

257.

TALK MAY BE CHEAP, AND I COME WITH A PRICE TAG

258.

TAKE TIME TO BE PRESENT IN THE MOMENT

259.

WHICH PIECE OF THE PUZZLE ARE YOU MISSING?

260.

YOU CANNOT DIVIDE AND CONQUER. UNITY IS THE ANSWER

261.

I CALL MYSELF A BIT OF A PROBLEM SOLVER, EX: X−U=ME

262.

I'M SWIMMING IN A SEA OF FOOLS TRYING TO STAY AFLOAT

263.

LOVE IS A GAMBLE. ANTE UP AND ROLL THE DICE

264.

LIES ARE LIKE ROCKETS, SOMEONE'S ALWAYS SHOOTING ONE OFF

265.

DAYS ARE A COIN TOSS, YOU WILL LAND ON EITHER HEADS OR TAILS

266.

PEOPLE ARE LIKE SEASONS. YOU SPRING FOR THEM. THEY CAN MAKE YOU HOT. THEN THEY MAKE YOU FALL FOR THEM AND LEAVE YOU ICE COLD.

267.

THE WAY TO A MAN'S HEART IS THROUGH THE KITCHEN (TO GET A BEER)

268.

THE WAY TO A WOMAN'S HEART IS WHEN SHE CAN REMOVE HER BRA

269.

I WISH THAT I COULD TAKE EVERY WORD BACK THAT I'VE SAID EXCEPT, "I LOVE YOU"

270.

OUR RELATIONSHIP IS LIKE A TRAIN WRECK; HOW CAN YOU NOT LOOK AT IT?

271.

I MUST BE ALLERGIC TO YOU BECAUSE YOU WHEN YOU HAVE NONE

272.

IT'S HARD TO WIN A BATTLE OF WITS WHEN YOU HAVE NONE

273.

ADVICE IS OFTEN GIVEN WHEN UNSOLICITED

274.

EVERY ACTION DOES NOT DESERVE A REACTION

275.

DO UNTO OTHERS BEFORE IT'S DONE UNTO YOU

276.

I SEE WHAT IT IS THAT I DON'T LIKE ABOUT ME INSIDE OF YOU

277.

IF IGNORANCE IS BLISS, WHY ISN'T THERE MORE PEACE IN THE WORLD?

278.

USE YOUR HEART AS A NET TO CATCH ME WHEN I FALL

279.

IF YOU'VE NEVER HAD A REAL FRIEND PERHAPS IT'S BECAUSE YOU DON'T KNOW HOW TO BE A REAL FRIEND

280.

YOU CAN CHOOSE YOUR JEANS, BUT NOT YOUR GENES

281.

LOVE YOUR BODY AS IT IS BEFORE YOU LOVE IT AS YOU WANT IT TO BE

282.

YOUR PERSONAL WORK IS THE MOST IMPORTANT WORK YOU'LL EVER DO

283.

NO ONE GROWS BY LIVING AN EASY LIFE

284.

I CANNOT SOLVE THE WORLD'S PROBLEMS, BUT I CAN ENHANCE ITS BEAUTY

285.

WHEN YOU GET TO THE ROOT OF YOUR PROBLEM, THE SOLUTION WILL BE EASIER TO FIND

286.

---◦◦◦---

THE DIRECTION YOU'RE GOING IS JUST AS IMPORTANT AS THE DIRECTION YOU'VE BEEN

287.

SECRETS ARE LIKE FLOWERS; THEY CAN POP UP ANYWHERE

288.

BE MINDFUL OF WHAT YOU FEEL AS WELL AS WHAT YOU SEE

289.

You never have to look for trouble

290.

MY CIRCLE OF LOVE IS BIG ENOUGH FOR YOU

291.

PEOPLE ONLY OF LOVE IS BIG ENOUGH FOR YOU

292.

You cannot get from the valley to the mountain without the climb

293.

THIS IS A DRAMA FREE ZONE

294.

THE PRICE YOU PAY FOR KNOWLEDGE IS IMMEASURABLE

295.

I WILL BE TRAINING FOR THE END ALL OF MY LIFE

296.

NO DREAM IS IMPOSSIBLE

297.

UGLY SEEPS FROM THE INSIDE OUT

298.

CHILDREN KNOW NO BOUNDARIES WHEN IT COMES TO THEIR CURIOSITY

299.

IF IT WAS EASY, I'D LET YOU DO IT

300.

WE ALL HAVE TWO CELEBRATIONS, BIRTH AND DEATH

301.

You must be able to follow directions in order to give them

302.

DON'T PUT PROCRASTINATION ON YOUR LIST OF THINGS TO DO

303.

MY GIVE A DAMN BUTTON IS BROKEN!

304.

IT TAKES LITTLE EFFORT TO MAKE A BIG DIFFERENCE

_____
_____
_____
_____
_____
_____
_____
_____
_____
_____
_____
_____
_____
_____

305.

USE YOUR VOICE AS A SIREN FOR CHANGE

306.

MAKE LIKE A SHOELACE AND LOOSEN UP

307.

RESPECTING YOUR SPACE ALLOWS ME TO STAY IN MINE

308.

THINKING LOGICALLY IS DIFFICULT FOR THOSE WHO THINK ILLOGICALLY

309.

BEING UNGROUNDED MAKES YOUR LIFE VERY SHAKY

310.

KEEPING YOUR HEART YOUNG WILL YOUR LIFE LONG

311.

YOU CANNOT EXTINGUISH A BURNING DESIRE

312.

NATURE IS THE MOST BEAUTIFUL IN ITS PUREST FORM

313.

THE PRETTIEST PORTRAITS ARE PAINTED BY (GOD)

314.

I HAVE TO LAUGH AT MYSELF BEFORE YOU BEAT ME TO IT

315.

PLAYING WITH SOMEONE WHO DOESN'T HAVE A FULL DECK CAN BE A DANGEROUS GAME

316.

APOLOGIES DON'T OCCUR ON THEIR OWN

317.

YOUR ENTIRE LIFE CAN CHANGE IN ONE SECOND

318.

I AM A WORK OF ART UNDER CONSTRUCTION

319.

I SPEND A LOT OF TIME TRYING TO REMEMBER WHAT I FORGOT

320.

I CAN ARGUE WITH THE TRUTH, BUT I JUST DON'T HAVE THE ENERGY

321.

LAUGHING IS AN INEXPENSIVE WORKOUT

322.

APPLES OR ORANGES. CAN'T WE ALL JUST GET ALONG?

323.

THE CHAPTER OF YOU IN MY BOOK HAS BEEN CLOSED!

324.

STRENGTH IS CREATED THROUGH WILL POWER

325.

BEING UNABLE TO BE YOURSELF IS EQUAL TO BEING IN PRISON

326.

BE BETTER. DO BETTER. LIVE BETTER.

327.

DON'T SAY THAT YOU WERE THINKING ABOUT ME BECAUSE I CANNOT SEE YOUR THOUGHTS

328.

SOMETIMES THE TRUTH STINGS LIKE A BEE

329.

PATIENCE ARE INKY DEALT WITH THROUGH PRAYERS

330.

STRESS IS CREATED WHEN YOU TAKE THINGS TOO SERIOUSLY

331.

I KNOW YOU'RE THINKING...... BECAUSE I SMELL SMOKE

332.

CHILDISH PEOPLE HAVE YET TO GROW UP

333.

KEEP YOUR CREATIVITY COLORFUL

334.

COMFORTING WORDS ARE GOOD MEDICINE

335.

FORGETTING TO BE GRATEFUL IS LIKE FORGETTING TO BREATHE

336.

REVENGE IS SERVED BEST COLD

337.

AGITATORS ONLY BELONG IN WASHING MACHINES

338.

IF I WANT TO PARTICIPATE IN THE FUTURE, I MUST TAKE CARE OF MYSELF IN THE PRESENT

339.

CHILDBIRTH IS A SCARY YET BEAUTIFUL THING

340.

BEING FASHIONABLY LATE REQUIRES NO SENSE OF STYLE

341.

TWENTY-FOUR HOURS A DAY IS ALL YOU GET TO MAKE A DIFFERENCE

342.

HAVE COMPASSION FOR YOUR COMPANIONS FOR THEY ARE NOT PERFECT

343.

RELIGION IS TAUGHT.
SPIRITUALITY IS FELT.

344.

You must humble yourself when you cannot do things for yourself

345.

CLOSE YOUR EYES AND ENVISION YOUR FUTURE. NOW OPEN YOUR EYES AND SEE THE POSSIBILITIES

346.

MEDITATE BEFORE YOU MEDICATE

347.

PEACE AND QUIET REQUIRE TWO THINGS, NO SPOUSE AND NO CHILDREN

348.

SLEEP IS WHEN THE BODY REPAIRS ITSELF. YOU CAN USE SOME REPARATION

349.

I CANNOT CARRY YOUR BURDENS BECAUSE MY HANDS ARE FULL OF MY OWN

350.

A CLOSED MOUTH DOESN'T GET FED AND NEITHER DOES A CLOSED MIND

351.

WHAT IF MISTAKES CAME WITH AN UNDO BUTTON?

352.

DON'T ALLOW YOUR HEART TO BE AS HARD AS YOUR HEAD

353.

Promise me that you won't promise me

354.

DO NOT DWELL ON THE DEATH OF ONE'S BODY, CELEBRATE THE LIFE OF THEIR SPIRIT

355.

TRAGEDIES ALWAYS HAVE BAD TIMING

356.

WHEN YOU ARE CALLED ON IN TIMES OF NEED, HOW WILL YOU ANSWER?

357.

SOME OF MY BEST TEACHERS HAVE BEEN CHILDREN

358.

YOU ARE GIVEN ALL OF THE TOOLS YOU NEED, WHAT YOU WILL BUILD IS UP TO YOU

359.

HAVE YOU EVER LOOKED AT YOUR REFLECTION AND ASKED YOURSELF, WHAT'S WRONG WITH THIS PICTURE?

360.

GREEDINESS ROBS YOU OF THE ABILITY TO "LET GO"

361.

BOUNCING IDEAS AROUND MAKES CREATIVITY BLOOM

362.

I WILL NOT HOLD YOU BACK, BUT I WILL HOLD YOUR HAND

363.

I HOPE TO INHERIT THE WEALTH OF KNOWLEDGE

364.

THE ONLY CONSISTENCY IS THE INCONSISTENCY

365.

CHOOSE YOUR CHOICES WISELY

www.ingramcontent.com/pod-product-compliance
Lightning Source LLC
Chambersburg PA
CBHW071919070526
44583CB00016B/2049